AEROSMITH
LIFE IN THE FAST LANE

MALCOLM DOME

Published by Castle Communications Plc
Book Division, A29 Barwell Business Park
Leatherhead Road, Chessington, Surrey KT9 2NY

Copyright © 1994 Castle Communications Plc

Design: Brian Burrows
Paintings/Illustrations: Brian Burrows
Photographs supplied by: Redferns, London Features International Ltd, Idols,
Bertrand Alary, Debbie Metal, APREF, Photofeatures International,
Fin Costello, Chris Walter, Steve Schofield, Mike Hashimoto,

ISBN 1-898141-75-4

CONTENTS

3

Aerosmith

Life in the Fast Lane

4   **MALCOLM DOME**

7

WELCOME TO THE SHOW

Aerosmith. The very word itself has become synonymous with Rock 'n' Roll over the past two decades. The origins of the name itself might be decidedly hazy and diverted by the onset of history, but there's no disputing the enormous impact made by the Boston band who have proudly taken their moniker to every corner of the globe, in the process setting standards few could ever hope to match.

Aerosmith are as American as John Wayne, Mom's Apple Pie and the Stars & Stripes. If the American football team the Dallas Cowboys have taken the epithet 'America's Team' over the years, then there can be little doubt that Aerosmith are worthy to be called 'America's Band' – brash, brazen, bold, belligerent and bombastic. Yet at the same time, they are capable of producing memorable music, in a style based heavily on the Blues, New Orleans Jazz and even Nashville Country. But underpinning it all is a sense of unique virtuosity and melody, with a streak of power and panache.

This is a band who have never dropped their standards, or indeed their guard. Throughout their turbulent history, they have constantly been in the public eye for more than just the music. They have been through more ups and downs than most. They have survived internal animosity and conflict on a level that would have destroyed lesser outfits – and indeed has. They have overcome line-up changes and upheavals. They have ridden through trends and fashions, always remaining one step removed from the storms of transient popularity. Aerosmith have retained credibility, whatever the prevailing musical climate.

In addition, the band have always been notorious for a deleterious addiction to every chemical excess known to man – and some that they seemingly invented themselves!

As vocalist Steven Tyler once wryly admitted, here is a band which probably kept the economies of more than one South American country afloat during the '70s, thanks to their unrequited habits. Most bands would have fallen apart under such pressures, but the 'Smiths just kept on rolling out the classic music, in the process establishing a rapport with the audience that meant that even during times of financial hardship in America, they could still sell out the largest of arenas.

And whatever criticisms can be aimed at this band, one cannot deny the enduring quality of songs such as 'Dream On', 'Walk This Way' and 'Toys In The Attic'. Numbers such as these, and many others, have ensured that Aerosmith have become one of the most influential and inspiring acts of all time. There are many successful, contemporary musicians who openly avow allegience to Aerosmith, admitting that without Tyler's gang they may never have formed a band of their own!

One such is Slash of Guns n' Roses, who has related on more than one occasion that hearing the 'Rocks' album changed his perspective on life forever, persuading him to take up the guitar and write his own chapter into the historical chronicles of Rock music.

This book is the story of Aerosmith, as told through their music and albums. It deals not with the sensationalist aspects of their career, but rather with the records, the songs and the music that has made them such an enduring legend in the annals of entertainment. It is a tale told through the eyes of a fan, yet also with the dispassionate eye of a critic. It charts the rise, the fall and the subsequent return in triumph of a band whom history simply wouldn't let slip into obscurity.

Aerosmith themselves once wrote 'Let The Music Do The Talking'. This to me lets the talking come through the music.

Thanks for their contributions in making this book
possible go to: Phil Scott, Nicola O'Donegan and all at
Castle Books and Penguin Books, Jo Bolsom, Sue
Brown and all at Geffen Records, Kerrang!, RAW,
Ultrakill! (and all associated with these magazines),
Lynn And Mark Putterford, Xavier Russell, Sylvie
Simmons, Arlett Vereecke, Sharon Black, plus many
others too numerous to mention.

This book is dedicated to the many millions of
Aerosmith fans across the world, who have kept the
flame burning – even during the bad times.

13

two

1970. A strange year in many respects. It marked the dawn of a new decade, and came accompanied (as with all fresh decades) adorned with a certain degree of optimism. However, it was also tinged with foreboding. The era of Flower Power was over, dead and buried 'neath the turmoil of the Sharon Tate murder, the fiasco that was Woodstock and the reality of the Vietnam war. Nobody believed anymore that merely wishing for peace and harmony was sufficient. Student protest marches had achieved little, save for media coverage and a sense of the protagonists being ill-equipped for life.

In Britain, it was the year when the Conservative party would be returned to government, under the leadership of Edward Heath. It was also the year when England's rein as the football world champions would end in Mexico.

15

Musically, this was the Summer when Jimi Hendrix died and many of the '60s groups found themselves incapable of reflecting the new realism pervading art in all its forms, as the '70s beckoned us forth. There was definitely room for fresher, harder-hitting acts. Hence the arrival of Aerosmith.

Born in the Summer of 1970, actually forming in the quaintly-named Sunapee, New Hampshire, the band originally took the slightly suspect name of the Hookers, thereby anticipating the sleazoid sexual innuendos in which many bands of that era were to indulge when choosing images and names. However, that particular moniker was inappropriate to this band, hence the change to the more esoteric Aerosmith.

"If you're the Hookers, you should come out looking like whores, y'know," said Steven Tyler years later. "So when we came across (the name) Aerosmith, it was great – it doesn't mean a thing!"

Tyler had begun life actually locked behind a drum kit, bashing away for the Jam Band, with Joe Perry (guitar) and Tom Hamilton (bass), among others. This trio were to form the basis for the 'Smiths, being joined by drummer Joey Kramer (taking over from Tyler, when he leapt forward to take control of the vocal duties) and, at first, guitarist Ray Tabano. However, Tabano himself soon vacated the band, being replaced by Brad Whitford. The birth of a legend was upon us.

Aerosmith soon built up a strong local following in their adopted home of Boston, their dirty, fiery Blues approach ensuring that they stood out from all their rivals and contemporaries at the time. The band took elements from Muddy Waters, the Rolling Stones, Led Zeppelin and even Iron Butterfly, melding and meshing them into a sound and style that soon gained the attention of record companies who were constantly seeking and searching for something fresh, original and enterprising. And it was Columbia Records executive

16

Clive Davis who won the fight for their signature, the latter being persuaded that this was indeed a band for the future after seeing a blinding set performed at the legendary club Max's Kansas City in New York. It was to prove one of the most inspired and important new signings of the early '70s.

In 1973 the band released their first album for the label in the US. Simply titled 'Aerosmith', the LP didn't even boast the seminal band winged logo. But the music was obviously of the highest quality. The cover itself had an ethereal quality, with the five members of the band being pictured against a sky backdrop. But there was nothing frilly or esoteric about the material on offer. For the most part, it was bruising, fired-up, harsh Blues, dirty at the edges and dragged through the gutter for that extra smell and sneer. If the Rolling Stones had laid the foundations for this type of Rock music, then Aerosmith were busy building their own edifice.

What's immediately obvious even now is just how vital and alive the music sounds. It may have been recorded on comparatively primitive equipment, but there was no disguising the swagger and steel. Here was a band anxious to get right to the top – and in a hurry to get there into the bargain.

Of course, as with most bands, this album effectively represented years of hard graft; from their inception right up to the recording sessions. The songs had been nurtured, honed down and stylised on the road – a luxury only afforded a band once in their career, ironically as they struggle to get out of the clubs and into the studio. And it's clear that the eight numbers here benefitted as a result.

"These songs had been our bread and butter for three years," says Perry, recalling those far-off days. And there's little doubt that when 'Aerosmith' hit the streets it stood out from the crowd for the most part

17

had a certain rough hew allied to a surprising maturity. At a time when most Rock bands were content to explore increasingly complex rhythmic patterns, and Progressive Rock was the term of the day, here was a group putting the emphasis clearly back on the basics. Simplicity was the key, coupled to a strong sense of melody and structure.

'Aerosmith' was issued in America during January '73 (a UK release date had to wait until October of the following year). And more than 20 years later, there are perhaps three tracks which stand out as worthy of further investigation, namely 'Walkin' The Dog', 'Mama Kin' and 'Dream On'. The first-named was a cover, being the 'Smiths' interpretation of a well-respected R&B standard, written by Rufus Thomas. Now, over the years many bands have put this particular track into their repetoire. The Rolling Stones even gave it their own individual attentions on their first album (not to mention the Flamin' Groovies and numerous others). However, in retrospect it is Aerosmith's approach that has become acknowledged as THE definitive version. Quite simply, it reeks of authenticity. The strolling gait of the backing rhythms, the winking, slinking guitar sashays from Joe Perry and, of course, Tyler's rasping, gasping throat...Add these factors together and you have a true blue classic.

A decade later, Los Angeles band Ratt were to do their version of 'Walkin'...' on their eponymous EP. Now, for a brief while, Ratt were regarded in some quarters – OK, I'll admit to being among the so-called cognoscenti on this one – as being the natural successors to Aerosmith. It never quite panned out that way. But when they recorded 'Walkin' The Dog', it was seen, and meant, as a tribute to Aerosmith. And, back then in the mid-'80s, if you'd asked most Rock fans who had first recorded the song, you'd have gotten one answer: Aerosmith. Such was the easy manner in which they made the song their own.

19

'Mama Kin' was arguably the first hard-hitting, bullet-to-the-head Aerosmith classic. It represented a style that over the years has been perfected almost to the point of genius by this band. Those who might criticize Aerosmith for their overtly simplistic approach to music have always missed the point. The band are entertainers, not sociologists. However, their lyrics have, more often than not, provided more balanced and attuned sociological statements than a million warblers crooning about the rain forests, or other such subjects of which they have no first-hand experience. Aerosmith sing and perform straight from the heart, using experience as a guiding hand. Thus, their songs are REAL, not just vehicles for musical dexterity. 'Mama Kin' was the first example of this.

What this song had was a cool power. It opens with a rush of chords and continues to fire on all available cylinders, with the underlying Blues trend never swamped by the sheer energy and aggression of the performance. This is essentially a Blues number – in both style and construction – but it also had a contemporary edge. Nobody who has heard this song can ever have been left in any doubt that this was more than just another cut on an album. No, this was a statement of future glories. As with 'Walkin' The Dog', many years later another top American band brought the song back into focus with their own interpretation. Guns n' Roses recorded 'Mama Kin' for their very first release, the 'Live Like A Suicide' EP. Their version (recorded live in 1986) owed much to the original and was more a paean to the brilliance of Aerosmith than it was just a cover version. Listening to the two closely, it easy to understand why Guns are regarded by many as closer to Aerosmith than any other band has come during the intervening years.

20

AERO

But if 'Walkin' The Dog' and 'Mama Kin' have become staples of the Aerosmith canon, then the last song mentioned has become arguably their enduring classic. 'Dream On' is to Aerosmith what 'Stairway To Heaven' has become to Led Zeppelin; what 'Sweet Child O'Mine' has become to Guns n' Roses. It is a masterpiece of balladry, proving to all and sundry just how one can combine the sharpness and power of classic Rock with a melodic beatitude and a calm, sensitive disposition.

'Dream On' begins with a gentle Mellotronic introduction, over which Tyler begins to croon, as only he can, with a plaintive, painful sense of reality and fantasy. Slowly, yet confidently, the song builds from this base into an inspirational elegy to love and loss. Even listening back to this very first commercially available recording of this classic, every aspect is in place. It sounds as vibrant and toned as it did way back in late '73, when I first heard it on vinyl.

Back in the dim mists of time, 'Dream On' became something of a minor hit on Rock radio stations across America. But, inexplicably it didn't hit the charts in any big way on its first release, reaching the hardly impressive peak of Number 59 in US. Maybe America simply wasn't ready for this type of single at the time; there was a certain sense in the rock world that the single record was something of a throwaway item, not the province for any serious Rock band. Thus, perhaps it was a compliment to the 'Smiths that they were regarded at the time in such a light. But, three years later, 'Dream On' was reissued as a single by Columbia. And this time, it hit hard – VERY HARD. The song became a Top Ten hit in the US, thereby establishing Aerosmith's reputation.

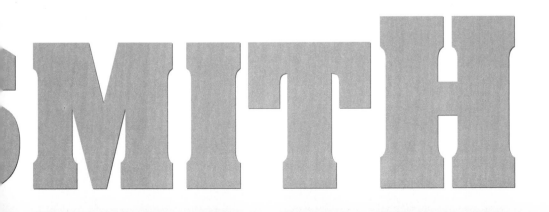

Aerosmith's debut album (produced, incidentally, by Cream/Vanilla Fudge/Allman Brothers collaborator Adrian Barber in Boston) sold steadily in the New Hampshire/Massechusetts area, but really didn't make much national impact. And on the international scene, it seemed as if the world wasn't truly ready for the style this band had to offer. They only attained cult status in the UK and Europe. But there was an irresistible force already on the move. Nothing was going to stand in this band's way. the future was there for the taking – and Aerosmith were planning to take their full share of the pie.

'AEROSMITH' (CBS 65486): 'Make It'/ 'Somebody'/'Dream On'/'One Way Street'/'Mama Kin'/'Write Me'/'Movin' Out'/'Walkin' The Dog'.

 **22**

ON A WING AND A PRAYER *Three*

Most American bands during the '70s (and beyond) found the best manner in which to establish themselves had been on the road. In such a vast country, one can tour and tour without repetition, slowly building up a huge following as one goes. Thus, a band may play club dates before no more than a couple of hundred interested parties per night when they first venture out, but given sufficient time and shows in all parts of the country, this can add up to a fan base approaching the tens of thousands, enough to create a chart position on the release of an album – and thence natural momentum (plus astute marketing nous) do the rest. This was the principle on which Aerosmith effectively worked.

"We couldn't get our stuff played on the radio. So we just had to get there and play," said Perry, revealing that this was indeed the manner Aerosmith chose to build their following up to sizeable proportions.

But one inevitability of such a gameplan is that writing material for any projected second album will suffer as a consequence. This was the situation facing Aerosmith as they prepared to record their second album, 'Get Your Wings'.

Using a combination of studio engineers; Jack Douglas (who was to become a crucial part of the band's subsequent successes), Jay Messina and Rod O'Brien, Aerosmith took the sound and style on their eponymous debut, and attempted to take everything a stage further. In comparative terms, it didn't seem to quite come off, although one must still bear in mind that, when we are talking in real terms, this is still an excellent recording, one that many lesser bands would have regarded as the pinnacle of their career.

23

"This was the point at which we began to write our material faster than before," says Perry of that period. "Our management (Frank Connelly, David Krebs and Steve Leber) decided that we should live together in an apartment, away from our girlfriends and other distractions and write. It had worked before, but this time it didn't really come off. But we had a good time doing it. I recall that what mattered most to us at the time wasn't getting on the radio or even having a hit single, but rather how things would work out onstage. That's what we lived for."

Looking back at the album now, it's obvious that in some ways the material was being written in order to recapture the same inspirations that had propelled the first record. Aerosmith were in danger of falling into the ill-starred trap of formularising a musical approach, that, by its very nature, should rely solely on attitude and instincts.

But, as I have previously stated, one can make the fatal mistake of being too critical of an album that still contained its share of top-notch offerings. Of the nine tracks put down, at least five have become popular and enduring items with Aerosmith fans. These are: 'Same Old Song And Dance', 'Lord Of The Thighs', 'SOS', 'Train Kept A Rollin'' and 'Seasons Of Wither'.

The opening cut 'Same Old Song And Dance' was an unfortunate choice in some respects. It gave critics the opportunity to have some fun by suggesting that what Aerosmith were indeed offering was the same old song and dance! A pity really, because this was a fine way to begin any album, being far from a repetitive number. Cut from the sturdy bark of perennial Rock 'n' Roll and Country Bluegrass, this was a strong track with immovable roots. The rolling, strutting base rhythms gave the band the opportunity to produce a forceful number filled with tension and flamboyance. Tyler is quite breathtaking as he leads from the front, taking the troops into an almost Big Band arena. Magnficent.

24

By contrast to the breezy, uptempo 'Same Old Song And Dance' came 'Lord Of the Thighs', a sleazoid, nudging pummelling groover that was both nasty yet, was also born of a certain naivety. This was a song of sexual gratification, sired on the road and thrusting its crotch right into your face. 'SOS (Too Bad)' and 'Seasons Of Wither' were similarly impressive in their own manner. And then there was 'Train Kept A Rollin''.

Yet another classic cover version, Aerosmith had almost certainly chosen to do this number because it had once been recorded by the English combo The Yardbirds, among the biggest influences on the band as they developed their style. Another Blues/R&B standard (written by Tim Bradshaw, Lois Mann and Howie Kay), it has become a staple encore number with many top bands over the years, and has also been recorded by the likes of Jeff Beck and Motorhead. A brilliant, rollicking cut that never relents, it was the perfect firebrand through which Aerosmith could spark and sparkle. And, whilst it has certainly not become as associated with this band as 'Walkin' The Dog', nonetheless it remains to this day a popular part of their live set.

In 1990, Aerosmith actually got two chances to perform this number onstage with one of their true heroes, guitarist Jimmy Page. Now Page may be known to most because of his role with Led Zeppelin, but he first came to the fore with the Yardbirds. Firstly at Castle Donington in front of 72,000 fans (standing in a field in the East Midlands of England), and thence at London's legendary Marquee Club (where The Yardbirds had made their name) before less than 1,000 fans, the 'Smiths played 'Train...' with Page, to the especial delight of the band themselves. On both occasions, it was a truly memorable experience. One perhaps that will never be repeated.

27

As with the debut effort, 'Get Your Wings' (which, incidentally, marked the first appearance of the famous winged logo on an album sleeve – albeit in a primitive form compared to the one so renowned and recognisable today) sold slowly. But all the hard roadwork that the band had undertaken was beginning to have its impact. Thus, by April 1975 (nearly a year after its release), the band finally achieved the coveted gold status for the record, reaching sales figures in excess of 500,000 copies in the US. Now, there could be little doubt that the band were on their way.

In conjunction with the fast-rising New York quartet Kiss, Aerosmith were about to become the hottest American act on the scene. Their next album had to be a masterpiece, capable of building on their incessant touring commitmnets and also one that could lift them several rungs up the ladder. It was all of that – and more!

'GET YOUR WINGS' (CBS 80015): 'Same Old Song And Dance'/'Lord Of The Thighs'/'Spaced'/'Woman Of The World'/'SOS (Too Bad)'/'Train Kept A Rollin''/'Seasons Of Wither'/'Pandora's Box'.

LIFE IN THE FAST LANE

28

TOYS, TOYS, TOYS!

For most Aerosmith fans, there is little doubt that the band's third album, 'Toys In The Attic', represented the start of a classic era in their heroes' history. It was recorded in early 1975 at the Record Plant Studios in New York (used previously by the likes of Led Zeppelin and the Stones), the fivesome were beginning to forge a remarkable partnership with producer Jack Douglas, one that was inspirational on 'Toys. . .'.

The album itself featured eight new original compositions, one of which ('You See Me Crying) was co-penned by Tyler with one Don Soloman, a former colleague of the singer's in a previous band called Chain Reaction (they had also worked together on material that appeared on the band's first two albums). In addition, there was yet another masterstroke cover version present in the form of Fred Weismantel's 'Big Ten Inch Record'.

The result was a cohesive unit of uniformly superb material. For the very first time, Aerosmith had focused their experience and talent, and as a result came up with something vibrant and voluble. The album opens with the title track, the first time that the band had actually penned a song with the same title as their album), a full-on belter of a number that represented arguably Tyler and Perry's best collaboration to date. It was a fiery beginning.

Following on from this came 'Uncle Salty', a much more sedate effort boasting a depressing tale of drugs and prostitution as its template. 'Adam's Apple' pulled everything back into an upbeart scenario, whilst 'Big Ten Inch Record' had a certain sleazy charm, complete with piano parts supplied by one Scott Cushnie. 'Sweet Emotion' was arguably the band's second

29

classic track on this album, building itself up from an almost whispered beginning into a chanting, grooving number that gyrated and thrusted with a sense of rhythm and timing that the band had not really explored before.

'Sweet Emotion' remains a 'Smiths masterpiece to this day. Its tale of underage lust and temptation being a theme Tyler, in particular, seems to enjoy exploring musically to this very day. It was actually the first single lifted from the album in the US. But perhaps the number that was to make 'Toys In The Attic' a true work of genius was none of the above, but rather 'Walk This Way'. If there is one number that perfectly sums up Aerosmith, then indeed this must be it. Over the years it has become a staple part of any Rock club's regular sounds and is instantly recognisable as soon as the opening hip-wiggling chords hit the deck.

'Walk This Way' is essentially a tale of lost virginity, a simplistic subject in itself but one Aerosmith gave added dimensions, thanks to the effective musical notations and adrenalin-pumped chorus, wherein Tyler screams and leers with zestful abandon. And over a decade later, it was this very song that was to play such a crucial role in letting a whole new generation know just what a potent force Aerosmith truly were.

By 1986, the 'Smiths had fallen somewhat from their lofty perch. A new style and sound had arrived on the scene through Rap/Hip Hop, appealing to young kids for whom the name and legacy of Aerosmith meant nothing whatsoever. Principle movers in this new movement were Run DMC from New York. When this trio elected to cover 'Walk This Way' for their 'Raising Hell' album, they invited the newly cleaned-out and reformed Tyler and Perry down to the studio to collaborate with them on a version. The Toxic Twins (as the pair were affectionately known) being asked to help out on the suggestion of Run DMC producer (and major Aerosmith fan) Rick Rubin. The recording sessions took five hours in all, and seemed to be an experience the pair hugely enjoyed. In fact, Tyler and Perry even took part in the accompanying video for the number.

This remake of 'Walk This Way' got to Number Four in the US (the 'Smiths' original had peaked at Number Ten a decade earlier), whilst it made Number Eight in Britain, the very first time that the band had ever gained a UK chart hit. Not bad for a song that came about virtually on the spur of the moment!

"It started out as a Joe Perry guitar lick and then I put my rhythmic lyrics, that stem from my early days as a drummer, on top," revealed Tyler years later. "I remember making up those lyrics the night we were meant to record the vocals. I wrote 'em on the walls of the Record Plant stairway!" Maybe all songs should be composed that way?!!

Upon its American release in April 1975, 'Toys In The Attic' quickly attained its own momentum, garnering critical and commercial acclaim as it went on its irresistible way. The record had surpassed the gold standard of 'Get Your Wings' by August '75 and went on to comfortably top the million mark, going platinum in the process. Jack Douglas had done his job exquisitly, and it seemed that his partnership with Aerosmith could only grow and grow.

"It was just an exciting time," said Joe Perry. "We were getting used to working in the studio. The shock of being in the Record Plant had worn off. We were getting into our own way of working with Jack."

AEROSM

By the end of
that year, Aerosmith
had achieved hits of
varying proportions with
'Walk This Way', 'Sweet Emotion'
and 'You See Me Crying'. And then
in December, 'Dream On' was re-issued
as a single. It was a master stroke by
Columbia. 'Dream...' became an instant
national radio airplay phenomenon, and this
time broke confidently into the US Top Ten,
reaching Number Six by the start of the next
year.

As a result of all this activity, not to mention the
constant touring (with Cushnie employed as a
backing musician), by the end of this period in their
career, Aerosmith not only stood proudly as the new
heroes of American arena Rock, but were also firmly
established as the biggest-selling artistes on
Columbia's roster. And when you consider that the
label also represented such diverse legends as Barbra
Streisand and Bob Dylan, then you get a measure
of this achievement! Perhaps only Kiss of the new
influx of major American Rock acts could hope
to keep astride of the runaway Aerosmith
bandwagon. Yet even they would have to admit
that, as 1976 dawned, Aerosmith were indeed
the Number One Rock band in the US.

'TOYS IN THE ATTIC' (CBS 80773):
'Toys In The Attic'/'Uncle Salty'/
'Adam's Apple'/'Walk This Way'/
'Big Ten Inch Record'/'Sweet
Emotion'/'No More No
More'/'Round And
Round'/'You See Me
Crying'

34

GET YOUR ROCKS OFF!

Five

In early 1976, on the crest of a wave, Aerosmith returned to the Record Plant and to the waiting arms of Jack Douglas to start work on their fourth album. It seemed something of an awesome task to try and follow up 'Toys In The Attic'. But Aerosmith were more than able to take on this onerous task. And the result was arguably an even better record in 'Rocks', which to this day is regarded by most Aerosmith aficionados as being their finest hour.

'Rocks' was released in the US during May 1976, and it quickly became obvious that almost every number contained in its grooves was a bona fide stroke of brilliance. The album opened up with one of the all-time great blockbusters in 'Back In The Saddle', which was to become the opening number for many a great Aerosmith live performance. Quite simply, it rumbles into life with an effectively raw savagery, before Tyler literally bursts through the mix, his voice sounding as though he'd just sandpapered his throat, and then gargled with wood alcohol. This was much more than a song – it was a statement of intent, throwing down the gauntlet to those who dared to cast envious looks at their crown as the Emperors Of Excess.

Following on from this comes 'Last Child', my personal all-time favourite Aerosmith number. There is a slight funky element to this cut, but also a sense of nascent streetwise energy and complexity. This song proved that, whilst lyrically, Aerosmith were very much stuck in the crotch region, nonetheless musically they could compete with anyone. 'Rats In The Cellar' returns everything to fever pitch, belting out the Rock riffs and rhythms over a tale of New York poverty. This was yet further proof, if any be needed, that when it came to revving up in the red zone, the 'Smiths were anybody's match.

35

Then there's the lugubrious 'Combination', written solely by Perry and something with an almost mystical bent to it. It many ways, this is one of the most challenging tracks ever cut by the band. To this day, it remains somewhat inpenetrable, but also has a magnetic charm all its own. By contrast the raunchy strut of 'Sick As A Dog' is pure Aerosmith bar room delivery, complete with a high wire instrumental ending that sees Tom Hamilton playing guitar, against the backdrop of a double barrel bass attack from Tyler and Perry. Jam session par excellence!

'Nobody's Fault' (a song inspired by the constant threat provided to California by the San Andreas Fault) was one of the heaviest numbers that the Bostonians had tried up until this point, whilst 'Get The Lead Out' cocked something of a snook at the Disco craze, proving that you can Funk it up without losing that sense of Heavy Rock credibility. It was a smoke-filled, rapid-fire blaze of Funk tones and Metallic sheen. 'Lick And A Promise', meantime, is simply stadium Rock incarnate. Tailor-made for the huge stage, it has such a big, brash, bold sentiment that it almost cruises up in a limousine with its arms around several groupies. Hell, you can almost smell sex'n'drugs'n'rock'n'roll in this little number!

Finally, everything came to a halt with the surprising 'Home Tonight', a sensitive ballad, wherein Tyler croons over the top of a huge 101-piece orchestra. A strange way to end an essentially upbeat album, but the tracking works to this day.

The result of all this activity was one of the greatest albums ever committed to vinyl. One that has stood the test of time magnificently. And one that was to have a huge influence on the next generation of Rock stars. The likes of Slash from Guns n' Roses and Nikki Sixx of Motley Crue both cite this record as the one that changed their attitude and lives. And there are millions like them the world over.

"This album and the one before set the template for all the different things we could do," states Perry with justifiable pride. "They showed that we weren't afraid to take chances."

"In essence 'Rocks' was the sequel to 'Toys In the Attic', and as such was really just a case of more of the same," adds Hamilton. "Except that it was harder, more exotic and a little more specialised. We were really at our peak at the time."

'Rocks' was certified platinum in the US upon release in May '76, and quickly went on to sell more than two million copies. And the band augmented this highly successful scenario by again hitting the road in America, playing the biggest gigs of their career. For instance, during May they played the 80,000-capacity Pontiac Stadium in Detroit, rapidly selling out the venue. And throughout the Summer, Aerosmith performed at a combination of large arenas (minimum capacity: 10,000) and stadia across their native land.

Moreover, in October of that same year, the band finally made it over to Europe, and they included four UK dates in their busy schedule. They appeared in London, Glasgow, Liverpool and Birmingham. But despite a huge media build-up, this tour proved to be less than successful. Reviews were, to say the least, rather mixed and tickets sold only slowly. Perhaps this wasn't completely surprising, given the fact that at the time, the combined sales of their albums to date in Britain hadn't even made five figures!

Further dates across Europe were equally disappointing, with the band eventually returning home in early November having lost a fortune. Their private plane alone had cost them £18,000 a night! When you put this up against net income of about £2,000 per night from shows, it becomes obvious why the band weren't exactly overly keen to return to these shores.

AEROSMITH

It was also at this time that the band were experiencing enormous drug problems. They were heavily experimenting, and whilst their music didn't seem to suffer in the slightest, nonetheless this was putting a huge strain on inter-band relations.

However, with the re-issued 'Walk This Way' hitting the US Top Ten singles charts in November and a hugely sucessful trip to Japan in early '77 under their belts, Aerosmith soon forgot about the European experience and began to look towards their next release. Could they follow 'Rocks'? Time would tell.

'ROCKS' (CBS 81397): 'Back In The Saddle'/ 'Last Child'/'Rats In The Cellar'/'Combination'/ 'Sick As A Dog'/'Nobody's Fault'/'Get the Lead Out'/'Lick And A Promise'/'Home Tonight'

LIFE IN THE FAST LANE

42

DRAWING STRENGTH

After a brief excursion to Japan, Aerosmith were finally accorded a well-earned rest by their management team (now Steve Leber and David Krebs). At last they had come off the album-tour-album-tour treadmill, and were given a chance to collect their thoughts and pen the strongest possible material for what was seen as a crucial record in the band's history.

For this fifth album, Aerosmith actually left the confines of the Record Plant and repaired to Upstate New York, being ensconsed with producer Jack Douglas in The Cenacle, a converted monastery. It wasn't exactly an easy time for the band, with recording only proceeding very slowly and stories emerging as to how the band's drug problems were, if anything, getting worse.

But during the Christmas period of 1977, 'Draw The Line' (as the LP was titled) finally emerged. It proved to be the biggest selling album in the band's history, thereby dismissing any thoughts that the quintet's popularity was on the wane. There were those who wondered whether the onset of Punk and New Wave music, through the likes of The Ramomes, Blondie, the Sex Pistols and The Clash, would sweep away Aerosmith as it had threatened to do to so many of their contemporaries. But nothing could be further from the truth. The plain fact was that the band had enough power, dirt and grit in their music to comfortably deal with any challenge from Punk. Their following was clear and committed. Mind you, 'Draw The Line' wasn't quite the classic we all hoped it would be.

43

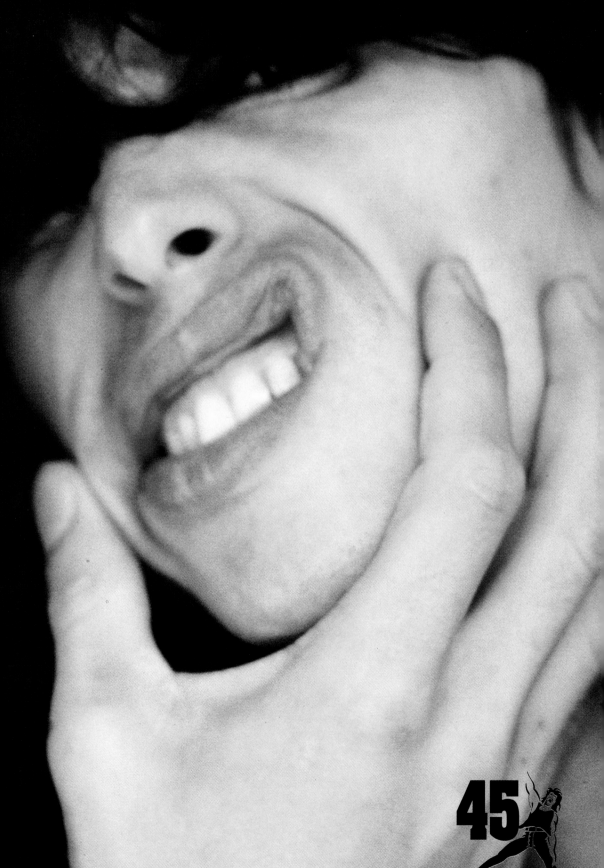

45

Maybe the band were suffering from something of a creative hiatus, brought about by the pressures of trying to match what had gone before. Perhaps all their chemical experiments were starting to affect their musical sensibilities. Whatever, 'Draw...' is a patchy affair. Certainly, the title cut and opening number promised much, with its classic Aerosmith hallmarks of quick-witted rhythm and blues-tinged firepower. Ironically, the band had chosen to unveil this track to the public a few months earlier when they returned to the UK to play at the Reading Festival. That day, it was clear that the song 'Draw The Line' was straight out of the top drawer.

Elsewhere on the record, 'Critical Mass' offers some semblance of order, with its brutal riffing and bombastic approach, whilst 'I Wanna Know Why' also proffers something of the true 'Smiths spirit, with its almost lazy groove. 'Kings And Quens' was a plaintive exposition, suggesting that it was to some extent a natural successor to 'Last Child'. On this particular tune, the band utilised a mandolin and banjo for extra texture. Meantime, 'Sight For Sore Eyes' returns to the funky elements the band so loved to explore.

But in with the goodies there were simply too many mediocre cuts. Certainly with the benefit of hindsight, Joe Perry admits that this album didn't quite cut the mustard.

"From the inside, I don't think anything was wrong. But from the outside you could see everything. You can hear the music getting cloudy. The focus we had on 'Rocks' is completely gone."

In the UK, there was still both commercial and critical resistance to the band, despite increased marketing commitment from the record label. However, Aerosmith just seemed to be getting ever bigger in America. Perhaps the biggest sign of their popularity came when they headlined the second ever Californian

47

48

Jam on March 18 1978, topping a bill that also included Heart, Santana, Ted Nugent (also managed by Leber and Krebs) and Mahogany Rush. There were an estimated 350,000 fans there that day, but it wasn't one of the band's more memorable performances. Drug excesses were really taking their toll, with the band even indulging backstage before playing their set. It was, to all intents and purposes, something of a mess.

Following on from this, the band agreed to appear in the ill-fated movie 'Sgt. Pepper's Lonely Hearts Club Band', playing the role of the Future Villain Band – the film's evil-doers. Yet, despite a cast list that also included Peter Frampton, The Bee Gees and Alice Cooper, this attempt at creating a monstrous Rock movie failed ignominiously. The film flopped, and the soundtrack fared little better. However, the enduring popularity of Aerosmith allowed their version of The Beatles' 'Come Together' (produced by long-time Beatles collaborator George Martin) to become a huge singles hit when put out in the US. It was the only Aerosmith contribution to the soundtrack record. But it is probably the best thing on that album.

Soon after their work on the 'Sgt. Pepper' project, the 'Smiths made what to some was a surprising decision to go back out on the road in the US, except this time they played under the pseudonym of Dr. Jones And The Interns at The Starwood Club in Los Angeles and The Paradise Club in Boston. These were to be the first of a proposed nationwide batch of low-key club gigs, the band wanting to get back to their roots. Sadly, the tour never happened. Instead, by the Summer they were back on the outdoor festivals trail, topping the bill at the first ever Texxas Jam on July 4 at The Cotton Bowl in Dallas (the bill also included Nugent, Mahogany Rush, Heart, Van Halen and Journey) before more than 150,000 people.

49

By this time, the soundtrack for the 'Sgt. Pepper' movie and an album featuring highlights from California Jam II (the 'Smiths contributed 'Same Old Song And Dance, 'Draw The Line' and 'Chip Away the Stone', the last-named never before available on an album) were in the shops, selling to a large extent on the back of Aerosmith's enormous and abiding popularity.

Aerosmith stayed out on the road in America throughout the latter half of '78, supported by AC/DC. And by the end of the year, the band had their first ever live album on the market.

'DRAW THE LINE' (CBS 821247): 'Draw The Line'/'I Wanna Know Why'/'Critical Mass'/'Get It Up'/'Bright Light Fright'/'Kings And Queens'/'The Hand That Feeds'/'Sight For Sore Eyes'/'Milk Cow Blues'

50

GIVE 'EM THE BOOT!

Seven

In November 1978, Aerosmith finally put out a long-awaited live album. It was a double effort titled 'Official Live Bootleg', which Tyler describes as "A great effort. I was getting ticked off seeing lots of bootlegs. Some of them had great covers, but no attitude, which is what we were all about. It was time to jump on it, so I had some rubber stamps made, we went up to the CBS art room and stamped out the logo on a piece of paper – and that was our sleeve design!"

'Official Live Bootleg' wasn't exactly a pretty affair. It lived up to its title by being genuinely a warts 'n' all effort. Most of the record was taken from various live tapes recorded over the previous two years or so, with a couple of special efforts thrown in for good measure. There was a version of James Brown's 'Mother Popcorn' taken from a show at Paul's Mall club in Boston, which is apparently the first club Aerosmith ever played at. Also included was a rehearsal take of 'Come Together', recorded at the Wherehouse in August 1978 (the Wherehouse being Aerosmith's own hideaway from the world). And there was also a version of 'Chip Away The Stone' included, a song written by friend Richie Supa.

But for the most part, what was included represented the band's live set at the time, which meant the rough edges were very much to the fore and there wasn't much sign of finesse anywhere to be heard. The album opens with a raucous and furious version of 'Back In The Saddle', the band sounding as if they were literally pumped on adrenalin and any other substance to hand. Tyler's vocals rasp and grate, yet sound dangerously electrified.

51

Following on from this comes 'Sweet Emotion' – the song surely never sounded so brazen and sleazy. 'Lord Of The Thighs' leads into a vicious version of 'Toys In The Attic', before 'Last Child' displays the band's punch without losing any semblance of emotion. Elsewhere, the likes of 'Walk This Way', 'Dream On', 'Mama Kin', 'Draw The Line' and 'Train Kept A Rollin'' maintain a very high standard of approach.

To many, the album was unpalatable simply because it hid nothing. During this particular period of time, the band were virtually out of control, Tyler would sometimes fall over during a set, completely dazed and confused by his drug addictions. In fact, he had to be carried onstage at some gigs, but once the lights hit and the music began to pump, Tyler would miraculously find his feet and range. Thus, one had to give the band enormous credit for not trying to hide behind studio technology and tarting up the tapes to make them seem more presentable. Many lesser acts would have done just that, but Aerosmith wanted people to hear them as they were – and the public in America loved 'em for it. 'Official Live Bootleg' went platinum upon release.

The band inevitably took to the road during the first part of 1979 in order to promote the album, but what 'Official Live Bootleg' had done is buy them some much needed time. They had to get their act together – and fast. Tyler and Perry were finding it increasingly difficult to communicate with one another, and this situation wasn't helped by their drug excesses. The question now being asked was could the band actually make it to the next studio album? As it turned out they did – but only just.

'OFFICIAL LIVE BOOTLEG' (CBS 88235): 'Back In The Saddle'/'Sweet Emotion'/'Lord Of The Thighs'/ 'Toys In The Attic'/'Last Child'/'Come Together'/'Walk This Way'/'Sick As A Dog'/'Dream On'/'Chip Away The Stone'/'Sight For Sore Eyes'/'Mama Kin'/'SOS (Too Bad)'/'I Ain't Got You'/'Mother Popcorn'/'Draw The Line'/'Train Kept A Rollin''

54

WHEN THE NIGHT FALLS

Having worked up a strong relationship with producer Jack Douglas, Aerosmith surprised many when they chose to record their final album of the decade with Englishman Gary Lyons (who numbered Foreigner, Humble Pie and Lone Star among his previous clients). Lyons acted as both producer and engineer on the new project, work being carried out at Mediasound Studios in New York. But it was to prove a fraught project for all involved. The process was lengthy and tiresome, with Tyler in particular proving to be difficult. In fact, Lyons ended up producing both 'Night In The Ruts' (as the band's seventh studio outing became known) and the new album from the Grateful Dead – at the same time.

What made matters even worse was that Perry walked out on the band in the middle of the recording sessions. Things had been approaching boiling point for some while, and finally came to a head in Cleveland, Ohio, when after a show, a band meeting ended up in a slanging match, with Perry electing to walk out on the band. Just how close Aerosmith actually came to splitting up at that point remains open to question. Certainly, the various members of the group were having severe personal problems. But they managed to soldier on, patching up the album and limping on. They considered drafting in UFO guitar hero Michael Schenker to replace Perry, but finally chose Richie Supa to put the final touches to the guitar parts.

"Joe Perry took his ball and went home," recalls Tyler of the split. "He also took his drugs and went home, which really pissed me off 'cos he had some great opium!"

55

The album was released in November 1979. Personally speaking, I have fond memories of it because it was the first time I got to write professionally about the band, reviewing said album for Record Mirror in the UK. I recall being very positive about it, awarding 'Night...' four stars (out of five). With hindsight, the album is very much underrated and something of a minor masterpiece. Considering the difficult circumstances under which it had been pieced together, this was a major shock.

It opens with 'No Surprise' (definitely one of Tyler and Perry's finest collaborations up until that point); the song relates the story of how the band fought their way to the top, which given just how close they had actually come to calling it quits during the 'NITR' sessions was ironic indeed! Elsewhere, the 'Smiths landed a few killer blows through the likes of the brassy, sassy 'Chiquita', 'Cheese Cake', 'Bone To Bone', 'Coney Island White Fish Boy', plus a very surprising cover choice, this being The Shangri-Las' 'Remember (Walking In The Sand)'.

The last named has been roundly criticised over the years by Aerosmith fans who believe it was a very misguided attempt. However, apart from being a bold move in itself (not to mention VERY left-field for this band), I feel that the years have treated the 'NITR' version kindly. It still holds up in the mid-'90s and certainly doesn't sound as cheesy and cloying as it could have been. Despite the severe problems being felt at the time by the band in general and Tyler in particular, there is something light-hearted and relaxed about this performance. It has humour and style.

Aerosmith's other two cover choices on the album were slightly more predictable: the first, the bluesy 'Reefer Head Woman', which was written in 1945 and was co-penned by the team of Lester Melrose, Joe Bennett and Willie Gillum. Altogether more in keeping with Aerosmith's natural sensibilities, this particular rendering is simple, harmonic yet also

57

fragmented. The other cover was The Yardbirds'
'Think About It', written in '68 by Keith Relf, Jim
McCarty and Jimmy Page. This one was more in
keeping with classic Aerosmith philosophy, the band
feeling right at home with a song by one of their
biggest influences. In fact, it's remarkable that The
Yardbirds were in a similar sense of disarray at the
time they recorded the original version of the
aforementioned song, hence perhaps the reason the
'Smiths were so able to recapture the spirit of the
original.

The man chosen to replace Perry was former Flame
guitarist Jimmy Crespo, who actually played a guitar
solo on the song 'Three Mile Smile' from 'Night...'
(although he wasn't credited at the time). The plan was
for the band to head out on the road in America to
coincide with the release of the album. But shortly
after that trek began, Tyler collapsed onstage in New
England – and all the plans were scuppered. The band,
it seemed, were on an inevitable course to self-
destruction. Tyler took to living in a hotel room in
New York, his health deteriorating as he indulged his
habits with wanton abandon.

A 'Greatest Hits' package released in October 1980
was the only sign of activity from the Aerosmith camp.
And amidst all of the inactivity, Brad Whitford quit in
the Summer of 1981. He had joined up with former
Ted Nugent vocalist Derek St. Holmes to form the
Whitford/St. Holmes combo during the hiatus in
'Smiths' activity. They made one self-titled album
with producer Tom Allom, which was released in
August '81. Shortly afterwards, Whitford decided that
he'd rather concentrate on this new project than wait
for any possible moves within Aerosmith. Perry,
meantime, was experiencing little commercial success
with his own band, The Joe Perry Project. He was to
record three albums with the band, beginning with 'Let
The Music Do The Talking' (released March 1980),
'I've Got The Rock 'N' Rolls Again' (June 1981) and
'Once A Rocker, Always A Rocker' (September 1983).

59

But with each release, Perry's record sales took increasing dives. Indeed, perhaps the sole legacy he has left is the track 'Let The Music Do The Talking', a song which Aerosmith themselves would record on the 1985 album 'Done With Mirrors'.

"I had written the basic tracks for 'Night In the Ruts'," Perry told journalist Sylvie Simmons at the time of his first solo release. "They were cut with as much lead as I could put in without the others. It was just taking Aerosmith so long to put that album out, and I was so fed up with that."

Years later, Perry summed up his feelings in retrospect thus:

"It was an era when I had to get away from the things that were starting to surround Aerosmith. I had to get back to playing music, playing clubs to see what Aerosmith meant."

But with Tyler, it seemed, intent on burning up in New York, Aerosmith surely were all washed up and finished? Not quite. By Christmas 1981, the band had found a new guitarist in Rick Dufay, to fill Whitford's shoes. Dufay had had a varied career up until that point, playing with bands like Modesty Blaise and Pegasus, plus releasing a solo album in 'Tender Loving Abuse', produced by Jack Douglas, who recommended him to the 'Smiths. Were the band's problems all behind them now?

'NIGHT IN THE RUTS' (CBS 83680): 'No Surprise'/'Chiquita'/'Remember (Walking In The Sand)'/'Cheese Cake'/'Three Mile Smile'/'Reefer Head Woman'/'Bone To Bone (Coney Island White Fish Boy)'/'Think About It'/'Mia'

ROCKING OUT THE HARD WAY

In an effort to get a new album completed, Aeromsith went into Criteria Studios in Miami with Jack Douglas to work on various ideas. They also rented a house in the city, installing a mobile studio there. But whilst material slowly emerged, the band still had problems with the wayward Tyler. In fact, so bad did things get that Crespo, Hamilton and Kramer actually laid plans for a new band in New York with singer Marge Raymond (an old colleague of Crespo's from his Flame days). Nothing was ever to come of this project, but to everybody's amazement, despite Tyler continuing to remain unpredictable, a new album was completed during 1982, with recording taking place in both Miami (at Criteria) and New York (Power Station). Three producers were used on the project, these being Tyler, Douglas and Power Station owner Tony Bongiovi. And if ever there was an Aerosmith album destined to be a disaster, then this was it. To everyone's surprise, however, 'Rock And A Hard Place' was quite brilliant.

If 'Night In The Ruts' saw the 'Smiths struggling just a tad, then 'Rock...' suffered not one jot from the attendant problems. Indeed, it remains one the band's best efforts. There wasn't a bad song on the album. Opener 'Jailbait' thrust itself into the spotlight with such verve and vivacity that it was clear that here was an Aerosmith who had effectively re-invented themselves. 'Lightning Strikes', meantime, was written by Richie Supa and is a swirling monster of a cut, full of epic bravado yet also vicious Rock 'n' Roll positivism. It's a track that became an instant favourite with, of all people, Joe Perry:

61

63

"It's one of my favourite Aerosmith songs," the guitarist said years later. "I was pissed off I didn't get to play on it, so I make up for it every night when we play it live!"

'Bitch's Brew' is equally as effective, almost burning its way through the speaker system, such is its fiery commitment. 'Bolivian Ragamuffin' is so raunchy it simply reeks of sexual innuendo, and the band's version of the famous Julie London cut 'Cry Me A River' once again shows their ability to pick surprising covers yet triumph despite the odds. This last named was actually recorded live in the studio – one take, no safety net.

'Rock In A Hard Place (Cheshire Cat)' returns the band to familiar big, brassy territory – scat Jazz with a wink and a nudge. 'Push Comes To Shove' has a certain late night charm, whilst the mysterious 'Joanie's Butterfly' brings with it a haunting, brooding sense of mystery and imagination that has since become a staple ingredient on all subsequent releases.

"This album remains one of my favourite albums," says Tyler. "But people didn't buy it 'cos Joe Perry wasn't there. Good! It's one of those records they'll buy and rediscover when we're gone."

The album was something of a commercial flop upon its release in October '82, although it did receive strong critical acclaim. Were Aerosmith fans really prepared to accept this change in line-up, especially the absence of Perry? The crunch would come when the band hit the road, when the world would see whether Tyler in particular could deal with the touring life, and being back in the public eye.

Prior to touring, though, the band were put through a real publicity gimmick, when they were persuaded to film three videos in 3-D, CBS believing that such a scam would really open the media floodgates. Thus footage for 'Bolivian Ragamuffin', 'Bitch's Brew' and

**64**

also for 'Sweet Emotion' was fimed in 3-D, rumours even abounding that this trio would do the cinematic rounds in support of the blockbuster movie 'Jaws III', itself shot in 3-D. The whole concept of three dimensional movies was back in vogue, and as promotional videos were also beginning to catch on, CBS reasoned that combining the two art forms would catapult Aerosmith right back to the fore. It didn't work.

However, when Aerosmith did finally take to the road in 1983, they found that the fans had not deserted them. Whatever the commercial problems faced by 'Rock And A Hard Place', they could still sell tickets in the biggest of American arenas. The band stayed out on the road into 1984, even playing huge festivals such as The Superbowl Of Rock shows in Florida on April 23/ 24. They headlined two dates over such other major acts as Sammy Hagar, Journey and Bryan Adams. But this line-up was to prove ill-fated.

When they set about trying to put down material for their next album, during '84, working in New Jersey and New York, they once again found problems with Tyler. And it became increasingly obvious that the only way Aerosmith were going to get anywhere was if Perry returned to the fold. The band needed the dynamic tension between the singer and the guitarist if they were to progress.

'ROCK AND A HARD PLACE' (CBS 85931):
'Jailbait'/'Lightning Strikes'/'Bitch's Brew'/'Bolivian Ragamuffin'/'Cry Me A River'/'Prelude To Joanie'/ 'Joanie's Butterfly'/'Rock In A Hard Place (Cheshire Cat)'/'Jig Is Up'/'Push Comes To Shove'

68

69

AB

MIRROR, MIRROR

By April 1984, the band were back in the saddle, with both Perry and Whitford back on board. The man given the credit for finally smoothing the path to a reunion between Steven and Joe was one Tim Collins, who had taken over the management of the Joe Perry Project and had become a close friend of the guitarist. Perry had even spent some time sleeping on Collins' couch. And just when it seemed that Joe would throw in his lot with Alice Cooper (the pair had even begun to write together), Collins eventually got him to speak sensibly to Tyler. The result was a welcome return to the fold for both Perry and then Whitford.

Collins, and his then-partner Steve Barasso, put the band out on the road for most of '84 and the beginning of '85. For the most part, they were welcomed back with open arms. The legend had returned – virtually intact and unshakeable. The new management also got the band out of their recording deal with Columbia and into bed with Geffen Records, the signing being completed by Geffen's top A&R man John David Kalodner. Thus, began the task of rehabilitating the band as a recording force.

They chose to work with producer Ted Templeman on their comeback trail. I recall meeting Perry and Tyler later that year in Boston on a balmy Sunday afternoon in a local restaurant to discuss their thoughts on the forthcoming new album ('Done With Mirrors'). They were an impressive duo, who seemed in complete control of their lives, with their old problems (both personal and pharmaceutical) behind them. Talking of Templeman's choice for 'Done...', Tyler said:

71

73

"We were looking around for possible producers when we heard that Teddy really wanted to work with us. He appeared at the Grammy Awards in Los Angeles earlier this year to pick up some prizes and was asked which band he'd most like to get involved with, and his answer was Aerosmith."

Templeman worked well with the band, even secretly taping what Aerosmith believed to be rehearsal run-throughs, in an effort to capture the essential spontaneity that had been such a crucial element in their success story. Eventually, 'Done With Mirrors' emerged for public consumption in August 1985. Yet, while many people were delighted to see the old band back in action, the album was something of a comparative commercial flop, selling less than half-a-million copies in the US – a real comedown for a band that had been used to a sales base of more than double that figure! What went wrong? Perhaps it had something to do with the absence of the band's legendary winged logo from the sleeve. A small point, but one that undoubtedly undermined the Geffen marketing stragegy, which saw everything printed as mirror images – too clever by half. Perhaps, also, there was feeling that technology and attitudes had left Aerosmith behind. They were in danger of being seen only as a harkback to the past. There was nothing for the Motley Crue fan of the mid-'80s to grasp.

But musically, 'Done With Mirrors' was a triumph. Opening up with the band's rendition of the old Joe Perry Project number 'Let The Music Do The Talking', they quickly hit their classic stride. 'Let The Music...' was always an Aerosmith stomper in all but name. Now here was the proof – a classic album kickstarter. 'My Fist Your Face' was equally as fired up, delivering Bluesy combination shots directly on target. 'Shame On You' had a slower, more smouldering groove to it, whilst 'The Reason A Dog' simply swung its hips and stuck out a leering tongue. 'Sheila' was a more mysterious affair, being almost balladic in texture, yet smothered in aural glitches. 'She's On Fire' was

another slow number, yet built on a virtually Jazzy torch song base – prime late night, smoke-filled bar fodder. And 'The Hop' was an uptempo joust.

Tyler himself was later to express disappointment in the album. And, perhaps, with hindsight, it wasn't strong enough on the production front. However, a live EP released in America early in 1986 suggested that the material should indeed be regarded as prime Aerosmith. Versions of 'She's On Fire', 'My Fist Your Face' (dedicated to the boxing champion Marvin Hagler) and 'The Hop' were breathtaking, as was a studio rendering of 'Darkness', left off the vinyl version of the studio album. There was, indeed, nothing wrong with Aerosmith's musical faculties. They just needed a little more enlightened guidance than had been provided by Templeman.

However, on the road Aerosmith were still attracting huge audiences. They set out in '86 on what was supposed to be a world tour. But exhaustion and debilitating physical conditions within the band eventually led to the whole trek grinding to a halt in May on the American leg. They were in desperate need of cleaning up. It was by this time a simple choice: clean out and get back to leading reasonably healthy lives, or run the risk of fatalities. They fortunately chose the former, which could not have been easy.

Tyler, in particular, went through the painful and slow process of rehabilitation, coming out of the other side ready to fire on all cylinders for the first time in more than a decade. However, whilst Aerosmith got their act together, the combination of old label Columbia and ex-management Leber-Krebs, hauled out some old live tapes, dusted them down and put out 'Classics Live' in April '86. It was a hotch-potch affair, tarted up in the studio, with additional guitar parts added in by Jimmy Crespo and Adam Bomb, the latter being managed at the time by Leber-Krebs (whose company was by then called CCC).

Of most interest here was the presence of a studio version of 'Major Barbra', which had never previously been available. Elsewhere, the choice of songs was obvious (ranging through 'Train Kept A Rollin'', 'Sweet Emotion', 'Dream On', 'Mama Kin' and 'Lord Of The Thighs'), yet this did little for the contemporary 'Smiths, being somewhat disappointing in sound and cohesion. But, with a video for 'Dream On' cobbled together from old footage, it was nonetheless a release that emphasised the classic quality of the band's legacy – and may ironically have done much to introduce them to a whole new audience, and to prove their influence on younger and hotter bands like Motley Crue and Ratt.

'DONE WITH MIRRORS' (Geffen GEF 26695): 'Let The Music Do The Talking'/'My Fist Your Face'/ 'Shame On You'/'The Reason A Dog'/'Sheila'/'Gypsy Boots'/'She's On Fire'/'The Hop'

'CLASSICS LIVE' (CBS 26901): 'Train Kept A Rollin''/'Kings And Queens'/'Sweet Emotion'/'Dream On'/'Mama Kin'/'Three Mile Smile'/'Reefer Head Woman'/'Lord Of The Thighs'/'Major Barbra'

IT'S HOLIDAY TIME, FOLKS!

Eleven

What might have happened in the Aerosmith camp if the follow-up to 'Done With Mirrors' had been a similar commercial flop one can only speculate on. Maybe it would have fragmented the band and led to a final split. Perhaps it would have made little difference. Whatever, this all remains in the realms of idle speculation, because that follow-up, 'Permanent Vacation', was to prove a huge success.

The band had initially wanted to work with producer Rick Rubin on the project. Tyler and Perry had gotten to know him well during the recording sessions for the Run DMC version of 'Walk This Way', as described earlier in this book. They even began work with him in February 1987, but other commitments for the producer meant that he simply couldn't give the band the time and space they needed. And this album was far too crucial to Aerosmith for it to be rushed.

Thus, attentions were turned towards Canadian Bruce Fairbairn, who made his name the previous year when he produced the hugely successful 'Slippery When Wet' album for Bon Jovi. That release had taken Fairbairn firmly into the very highest echelons of producers and made him a much-wanted man. He was the right man to work with Aerosmith because they desperately needed somebody on board with a contemporary attitude. Moreover, on the songwriting front, Kalodner elected to bring in such top composers as Desmond Child (another man with Bon Jovi connections), Jim Vallance (long-time partner with Bryan Adams) and the peripatetic Holly Knight.

79

The result, when issued in August 1987, was an album full of the old 'Smiths traits, yet one blessed with sufficient late '80s touches to make it appealing to a wide audience. The months spent in Little Mountain Studios, Vancouver, working on this platter were more than rewarded as this record quickly outsold 'Done With Mirrors', going on to sell more than five million copies in the US alone. It even made the UK charts – the first time the band had actually achieved such a position.

'Permanent Vacation' is without doubt a classic album of its time. Filled with all the elements which had combined to make the 'Smiths such a legend in the first place, yet also polished and stylish enough to make it easily accessible to a new generation used to high-tech performance. This was an album for the Compact Disc age.

Opening up with the heatbeat of two killer whales (there was even a motif on the back of the album in support of Greenpeace), this slips easily into the busy and infectious 'Heart's Done Time'. From hereonin, it's a rollercoaster of excitement and melody. 'Magic Touch' is Pop-Rock at its best, whilst 'Rag Doll' harks back to the old days of Blues workouts, and 'Simoriah' continues the band's habit of going for off-the-wall rhythms. 'Dude (Looks Like A Lady)', the first single from the album, is simply ebullient sleaze with a gruelling backbeat breaking sweat, as Tyler delivers one of his best ever vocal performances. This was the first single to be lifted from the album, reaching Number 14 in the US, and even making the Top 40 in the UK, the band's first ever solo showing in the UK singles charts.

LIFE IN THE FAST LANE

'Hangman Jury' and 'St. John' are pure Blues banner wavers, whilst 'Girl Keeps Coming Apart' returns to Pop-Rock territory, and 'Angel' is the best type of Rock power ballad. The title track itself has an almost Calypso beat to it, whilst the band's version of The Beatles' 'I'm Down' adds yet more lustre to their growing canon of supreme covers. Finally, there was the haunting instrumental 'The Movie', which was originally to be included on the 'Done With Mirrors' set.

Talking about the album, Tyler enthused: "Everybody's flipped over the record, and the reason why it's so much better than the last album is that we did it straight. With the last one we'd come up with a guitar riff and then we'd be off into the bathroom snorting like assholes. But this time we gave it 101 per cent – and it shows! Every rehearsal we did for 'Permanent Vacation' was like a show!"

Overall, 'Permanent Vacation' was the album for the time. Backed up by promotional videos which showed that the band looked better than ever, it was no surprise to see it proving such an enormous success. And cleaned up and sharper than ever, the band were eager and anxious to hit the road. They finally got their wish in October, when they began touring once more. Strangely, Aerosmith were supposed to come to the UK the previous month for a tour wherein they'd have been supported by Guns n' Roses. Tickets had even gone on sale, but then the tour was pulled, with Tyler enigmatically explaining that "Somebody in Sweden had fucked up!" Hmmm.

But, with the album selling like crazy in the US, it seemed that they just wanted to concentrate on the world's biggest market. They stayed out on the road until September 1988, playing arenas, stadia and festivals with a huge variety of bands. On their own headlining dates, Aerosmith were supported by the likes of Dokken, White Lion and Guns n' Roses. In The Summer of '87, they played second on the bill to

83

Boston at the Texxas Jam in Dallas (Whitesnake and Poison were among the bands below them on the bill). In August 1988, the 'Smiths headlined at Giants Stadium in New Jersey, with Deep Purple and Guns n' Roses as the supporting cast. Aerosmith were back – and this time they didn't have the heavy baggage of drug problems hanging over them!

In June 1987, the band had also been involved in another album release, this being 'Classics Live II', a follow-up to the patchy 'Classics Live'. The difference between the two was that, whilst Aerosmith themselves had not taken part in the first release, they were persuaded to get involved in the latter. It also brought them back in the contact with former manager David Krebs and also Columbia Records.

'Classics Live II' was all the better for the band's involvement. They even delved into their own tapes to find quality performances. The album opens with 'Back In The Saddle' and continues at a very high level through such monsters as 'Walk This Way', 'Same Old Song And Dance', 'Last Child', 'Let The Music Do The Talking' and 'Toys In The Attic'. So, as the decade rumbled out, Aerosmith's stock stood higher than ever before. Things could only get better – and they did!

'PERMANENT VACATION' (Geffen WX 126): 'Heart's Done Time'/'Magic Touch'/'Rag Doll'/ 'Simoriah'/'Dude (Looks Like A Lady)'/'St. John'/ 'Hangman Jury'/'Girl Keeps Coming Apart'/'Angel'/ 'Permanent Vacation'/'I'm Down'/'The Movie'

'CLASSICS LIVE II' (CBS 460037): 'Back In The Saddle'/'Walk This Way'/'Movin' Out'/'Draw The Line'/'Same Old Song And Dance'/'Last Child'/'Let The Music Do The Talking'/'Toys In The Attic'

PUMP UP THAT VOLUME

Twelve

I t didn't take long after finishing up on the road, for the band to get going on ideas for their next album. And by January 1989, they had the songs ready to roll. Thus, the whole shebang relocated to Vancouver again, with the band ensconsing themselves in Little Mountain Studios once more, with Fairbairn accepting for the second time the position of Master Of Ceremonies.

What emerged was far from being 'Permanent Vacation Part II'. No, with Tyler particularly concerned that the band might just have gone a little bit too far in the direction of commercial compromise on 'PV', this time around they went for a more esoteric, even ethnic, delivery.

"I'm scared to death of ever becoming as big as Bon Jovi," the singer said soon after the release of 'Pump'. There's something that scares me about being successful and having my face all over MTV. There's a part of me that says that's wrong and fucked up. Maybe it just goes to show my old Rock 'n' Roll roots.

"With this new album, we've taken such a risk by throwing weird shit in there from all over the place."

What 'Pump' has is a remarkable cohesion. Whilst not a concept album as such, nonetheless there are no gaps between tracks, but there are musical vignettes acting as links between songs. These draw on Zydeco and Cajun music, even African rhythms. The result is something of an epic, and arguably the band's finest release since 'Rocks'.

The inter-song interludes owed much to a collector of unusual instruments called Randy Raine Reusch.

87

88

"Joe and I bumped into him in Vancouver. He had a collection of instruments from all over the world. He had a room with hundreds, maybe thousands of them," explained Tyler. "Little bamboo things, big bamboo things, stuff made from human femurs, weird things from all over. He just brought everything that we picked out down to the studio and let us jam with them, and what we came up with, we used as interludes to tie the whole album together."

Thus, the band ended up with strange notations on such tracks as 'Don't Get Mad, Get Even'. And the intro to the song 'Voodoo Medicine Man' was inspired by tapes of African rituals borrowed by Tyler from Guns n' Roses guitarist Izzy Stradlin during the '88 tour.

However, this was far from being just a collection of weird and wonderful ethnic rhythms. Desmond Child was brought into add his silver touch to the songs 'F.I.N.E.' (which apparently stands for 'Fucked up, Insecure, Neurotic and Emotional) and 'What It Takes'; whilst Jim Vallance had a hand in 'The Other Side' and 'Young Lust'.

In September 1989, the new album was released to ecstatic approval. Commercially, it proved to be another huge seller for the band. It was a top five effort in the US charts, and went even closer to the top spot in the UK. The previous month, the first single from the album, 'Love In An Elevator', had reached Number 13 in Britain, whilst breaking through the Top Five in America.

'Pump' is an excellent album, which might well be regarded as the conerstone of the band's later works. Opening with the hormonally pumping 'Young Lust', it doesn't let the foot off the peddle for 'F.I.N.E.', whilst the tongue-in-cheek sexuality of 'Love In An Elevator' can't fail to bring a smile to the face, Tyler's innuendo-etched lyrics warming to the task.

91

AERO

 92

'Janie's Got A Gun' is an altogether more moody and serious aspect, dealing with the very sensitive subject of family sexual abuse – the accompanying video being painfully harrowing. 'The Other Side', however, soon lifts the tempo and gets the spirits right back up, whilst 'Don't Get Mad, Get Even' doesn't spare the rod or the whip, blowing out real invective.

What makes 'Pump' such a joy to behold is the musical versatility that it shows throughout. No avenue's too dark or dangerous to explore. Yet, Fairbairn's production holds the entire body of work together, stopping it short of becoming too cluttered and jumbled.

Tyler also took time out to contribute some backing vocals to a track from Motley Crue's 'Dr. Feelgood' album, being recorded at Little Mountain Studios during the same period that the 'Smiths were working on 'Pump'. Tyler also sponsored Crue bassist Nikki Sixx's introduction to Alcoholics Anonymous, an organisation which had led the Aerosmith legend in his own transition to sobriety.

Touring-wise, this time around the band chose to begin in Europe, finally making it to the UK in October for a series of ecstatically-received sold-out dates. These included a stint at the famous Hammersmith Odeon; the second night of which saw Whitesnake vocalist David Coverdale join the band for an encore rendition of 'I'm Down'. The band looked leaner, smarter and sharper than ever; revelling in their new-found health. After the Euro-trek, Aerosmith took to the road in America for a gruelling period of touring in support of 'Pump'. And they were still going strong when they returned to the UK on August 18 1990 to play at the legendary Castle Donington Monsters Of Rock festival.

95

The band were special guests on the bill, below the headlining Whitesnake and above such acts as Poison, the Quireboys and Thunder. It was to prove something of a triumphant return for Tyler and the boys. Jimmy Page, as mentioned earlier, even found time to get up and jam with the band on 'Train Kept A Rollin''. Two days later, Aerosmith played to a packed Marquee Club audience, bringing the house down during a six-song encore liason with Page, including such Yardbirds standards as 'Think About It' and 'Ain't Got You'; not to mention Led Zeppelin's 'Immigrant Song' and the inevitable 'Train Kept A Rollin''. Aerosmith were no longer merely an American act, with pockets full of cult followers throughout the world. They were now major news everywhere.

'PUMP' (Geffen WX 304): 'Young Lust'/'F.I.N.E.'/ 'Going Down'/'Love In An Elevator'/'Monkey On My Back'/'Water Song'/'Janie's Got A Gun'/'Dulcimer Stomp'/'The Other Side'/'My Girl'/'Don't Get Mad, Get Even'/'Hoodoo'/'Voodoo Medicine Man'/'What It Takes'

97

GRIPPING YARNS

By 1992, Aerosmith were back at work on yet another new album. Only this time, although Bruce Fairbairn was once more involved, they moved studios from Little Mountain to A&M in Los Angeles.

"We needed to go somewhere else away from Vancouver this time," Tom Hamilton said, while the band were working on the record. "All of us in the band felt that we needed a change of pace and scene. And for a short period of time, it did look as if we'd have to change producers as a result. We had a chilly meeting with Bruce about the situation, after which there did seem the possibility that we wouldn't be working with him. He was far from happy with the things that we were proposing, and we in turn weren't very impressed with his attitude."

However, while there might have been a degree of friction between Fairbairn and Aerosmith, tempers cooled over a period of time, and Fairbairn agreed to the band's proposal to move studio locations.

"For a while it was fun for us to pretend to be residents in Los Angeles," admitted Hamilton. "But the purpose behind the change of studio and city didn't work out."

The band recorded some 14 songs at A&M, but nobody seemed satisfied with the standard and quality achieved at this juncture. Reports emanating from various sources suggested that Aerosmith had actually completed the album - or at least that they thought that they had, until the powers-that-be at Geffen decided that the material was simply not ready for release. So, they told the 'Smiths to go back into the studio and improve the product.

"We know that we can do better," was Hamilton's assessment of the situation. "And we are lucky in the fact that we are at a stage in our career when we can take the extra time we need to get something right."

So, the band returned to Little Mountain to carry out the extra work required on the album.

"We will keep on going until we believe we have the right follow-up to 'Pump'," Hamilton stated, whilst Aerosmith were still ensconsed in the studio. "For us, this second stage in the recording process represents a new cycle in the album process. We have been improving on some of the things that we've already done, because we know it's possible. In the past, we've listened back to albums after they were finished and known there were certain things which could have been improved. Now, we've got the chance to do exactly that before release!"

When the record did finally appear in the Spring of '93, it was titled 'Get A Grip', but although it sold briskly, it received something of a muted critical response. It just wasn't as impressive or inspirational as either 'Permanent Vacation' or 'Pump'. Put succinctly, it sounded too produced; as if some of the band's spirit had been squeezed out as a result. It didn't quite gel.

But there are some tremendous moments nonetheless. First single 'Livin' On The Edge' has a rolling melodic feel, with a richly resonant chorus. And the accompanying video was strikingly visual, with Tyler himself being made up in a daring and distinctive style. Who could forget the moment in the video when Perry undertakes a livid solo while standing on railway tracks – a train thunders towards him! And the moment when he nonchalantly steps off the rails, just as the train fires past, epitomises the coolness of the man!

Elsewhere on the record, 'Cryin'' is another fine ballad, while 'Eat The Rich (featuring a Polynesian drum troupe) is a vibrantly textured rocker. The band also brought in a number of guests to perform on the record. Lenny Kravitz plays guitar on 'Line Up', and Richie Supa contributes some guitar to his composition, 'Amazing'. The same number also has former Eagle Don Henley on backing vocals. Desmond Child co-wrote 'Crazy' and also played piano on the track; while Damn Yankee duo Jack Blades and Tommy Shaw helped in the penning of 'Can't Stop Messin''. Yet, overall the feeling was that Aerosmith had slipped slightly from their lofty perch - although by most others' standards this was still a magnificent effort.

The subsequent touring schedule has seen the band traversing the globe once more. They were also accorded the honour of headlining at the Castle Donington Monsters Of Rock festival on June 4, 1994; thereby joining Rainbow, AC/DC, Status Quo, Whitesnake, ZZ Top, Ozzy Osbourne, Bon Jovi and Iron Maiden in the elite pack of artists that have topped the bill at Britain's biggest rock festival. They were joined on this particular bill by the likes of fellow Bostonians Extreme; Sepultura, Pantera and Therapy?. And it is a measure of the band's ability to appeal to Rock fans both old and new that they could headline such a diverse bill.

So, wither Aerosmith as we approach the last few years of the millenium? Well, in late 1991 the band signed a new recording deal which will see them returning to Columbia. But this was one of the most unusual deals of recent times, because the band still owed Geffen two albums at the time. It could be 1996 before their last contractual obligation to Geffen is discharged and the next studio album is forthcoming. If that is the case, then who knows, we could be looking at the year 2000 before the band deliver a new studio recording to Columbia, in time for their 30th anniversary!

On stage with 'guest' Jimmy Page at London's famous Marquee Club

LIFE IN THE FAST L
AEROSMI

AEROSMITH
IN THE FAST LANE

105

"We've managed to get ourselves to a level as a group where a record company can readily accept such a deal," explained Hamilton when the rumoured eight-figure deal was signed. " It's a vote of confidence in us. Of course, you never know what can go wrong, but I've a feeling we'll have an album out for Columbia before 2000!"

Still, shortly after signing that deal, Columbia did get some product out of the 'Smiths, with the release of the 'Pandora's Box' set, featuring rare versions of established songs and previously unreleased material. It was a timely reminder of just how much Aerosmith have influenced the development of Rock music over the past two decades. And doubtless, the band will continue to dominate the scene for many years to come.

'America's band'? Hardly the case any more in these descriptive times. More like 'A Global Band'. Perhaps they could even now be called 'The Greatest Rock 'n' Roll Band In The World!!!'.

'GET A GRIP' (Geffen GEF 24444): 'Intro'/'Eat the Rich'/'Get A Grip'/'Fever'/'Livin' On The Edge'/ 'Flesh'/'Walk On Down'/'Shut Up And Dance'/ 'Cryin''/'Gotta Love It'/'Crazy'/'Line Up'/'Can't Stop Messin''/'Amazing'/'Boogie Man'

On stage with
Jon Bon Jovi
at L.A. Forum

APPENDIX

Apart from all the albums listed in this book, Aerosmith have also had a number of compilations released. These are as follows:

'GREATEST HITS' (CBS 84704): 'Dream On'/ 'Same Old Song And Dance'/'Sweet Emotion'/'Walk This Way'/'Last Child'/'Back In The Saddle'/'Draw The Line'/'Kings And Queens'/'Come Together'/ 'Remember (Walking In The Sand)'

'ANTHOLOGY' (Raw Power RAWLP 037): 'Toys In The Attic'/'Sweet Emotion'/'Walk This Way (live)'/ 'No More No More'/'You See Me Crying'/'Bright Light Fright'/'Lord Of The Thighs'/'Back In The Saddle (live)'/'Sick As A Dog'/'Critical Mass'/'The Hand That Feeds'/'Sight For Sore Eyes'/'Mother Popcorn'/'Train Kept A Rollin''/'SOS (Too Bad)'/ 'Rock In A Hard Place'/'Jailbait'/'Push Comes To Shove'/'Rats In The Cellar'/'Bone To Bone'/'Dream On'

'GEMS' (CBS 463224-2): 'Rats In The Cellar'/'Lick And A Promise'/'Chip Away The Stone'/'No Surprise'/ 'Mama Kin'/'Adam's Apple'/'Nobody's Fault'/'Round And Round'/'Critical Mass'/'Lord Of The Thighs'/ 'Jailbait'/'Train Kept A Rollin''

'GRIPPING STUFF' (Geffen promotional release. Never commercially available): 'Let The Music Do The Talking'/'My Fist Your Face'/'Rag Doll'/]Dude (Looks Like A Lady)'/'Angel'/'Going Down'/'Love In An Elevator'/'Water Song'/'Janie's Got A Gun'/ 'Dulcimer Stomp'/'The Other Side'/'What It Takes'/ 'Eat The Rich'/'Livin' On The Edge'/'Cryin''/ 'Amazing'/'Line Up'/'Crazy'

'PANDORA'S BOX' (CBS): A collection of rarities and previously unreleased material

III

112